Dear Parents and Teachers,

In an easy-reader format, **My Readers** introduce classic stories to children who are learning to read. Nonfiction **My Readers** tell true stories and convey fascinating facts to children who are ready to read on their own.

My Readers are available in three levels:

1 **Level One** is for the emergent reader and features repetitive language and word clues in the illustrations.

2 **Level Two** is for more advanced readers who still need support saying and understanding some words. Stories are longer with word clues in the illustrations.

3 **Level Three** is for independent, fluent readers who enjoy working out occasional unfamiliar words. The stories are longer and divided into chapters.

Encourage children to select books based on interests, not reading levels. Read aloud with children, showing them how to use the illustrations for clues. With adult guidance and rereading, children will eventually read the desired book on their own.

Here are some ways you might want to use this book with children:

- Talk about the title and the cover illustrations. Encourage the child to use these to predict what the story is about.
- Discuss the interior illustrations and try to piece together a story based on the pictures. Does the child want to change or adjust his first prediction?
- After children reread a story, suggest they retell or act out a favorite part.

My Readers will not only help children become readers, they will serve as an introduction to some of the finest classic children's books available today.

—LAURA ROBB
Educator and Reading Consultant

For activities and reading tips, visit myreadersonline.com.

SQUARE
FISH

An Imprint of Macmillan Children's Publishing Group

SEAL PUP RESCUE. Text copyright © 2013 by Brenda Peterson.
Photographs copyright © 2013 by Robin Lindsey, except
image of pug on p. 14 © iStockphoto.com/falcatraz.
All rights reserved. Printed in China by Toppan Leefung Printing Ltd.,
Dongguan City, Guangdong Province.
For information, address Square Fish, 175 Fifth Avenue, New York, NY 10010.

Library of Congress Cataloging-in-Publication Data Available

ISBN 978-1-250-02775-7 (hardcover)
1 3 5 7 9 10 8 6 4 2

ISBN 978-1-250-02776-4 (paperback)
3 5 7 9 10 8 6 4 2

Book design by Patrick Collins/Véronique Lefèvre Sweet

Square Fish logo designed by Filomena Tuosto

Originally published in similar form as *Leopard & Silkie*
by Christy Ottaviano Books, an imprint of Henry Holt and Company, 2012.
First MY READERS Edition: 2013

myreadersonline.com
mackids.com

This is a Level 2 book

Lexile 570L

Seal Pup Rescue

Brenda Peterson

photographs by **Robin Lindsey**

SQUARE FISH

Macmillan Children's Publishing Group
New York

Leopard is born at sunrise
on a summer day.

He is a golden, spotted seal pup.

Leopard is shorter
than a skateboard
and weighs a little more
than a bowling ball.

Leopard's white and wavy fur
looks dark when it's wet.
Leopard nuzzles
with his mother.
Then he drinks a bellyful
of rich milk.

His mother learns

her pup's scent and sounds

so she can find him

when they are apart.

Leopard explores the beach.

He uses his foreflippers

to hop and slide

along the sand.

Leopard is only one hour old,

but it's time

for his first swimming lesson.

"Maaaaa!" he calls.

Leopard plays in shallow rock pools.

When he gets tired,

he catches a ride

on his mother's back.

Leopard naps in a secret cove
while his mother fishes nearby.
Is Leopard safe?

Yes, he is.

Miles is watching.

Miles is a Seal Sitter.

Seal Sitters help protect seal pups.

Miles knows it's natural

for pups like Leopard to nap onshore.

The sea is cold,

so pups warm up on the beach.

The next day,

Leopard is alone onshore,

waiting for his mother.

The beach is filled with people.

They look like giants to Leopard.

They come too close

and talk too loud.

"Is the seal dead?" children ask.

"Where is the mother?"

Leopard is very scared.

He has never seen people before.

Will they hurt him?

Will they steal him from the beach?

Leopard shivers

and covers his face to hide.

"Please, stand back!" says Miles.

"This pup is just resting.

The mother may be watching us

from the water."

Miles asks people

to put their dogs on leashes.

Then Miles puts up

yellow tape around Leopard.

It reads "Protected Marine Mammal."

This keeps people away

from Leopard.

They can watch him
with their binoculars.
Leopard rolls on his back and yawns.
He even falls asleep.

Soon Miles has another idea.

He helps build a large raft

of plywood and foam.

A floating island!

Leopard can rest there

when the beach gets crowded.

Other Seal Sitters

help watch over Leopard

until the raft is finished.

Miles and other Seal Sitters
row out with the raft
into the cold waves.
He ties the raft to a buoy
just offshore.

But Leopard does not leave the beach.
Is he too scared to swim
out to the raft by himself?

Miles waits
and worries.

Suddenly, a head appears
in the waves.
"Maaaaa!" Leopard cries,
and he flop-hops
from the beach into the surf.

Then Leopard and his mother

leap up onto the raft!

The seals wave and flap their flippers.

Leopard and his mother

swim together.

Leopard learns how to catch fish.

Then they relax with friends.

Now Leopard has

a safe place to sleep

while his mother is away.

Leopard sleeps and dreams,

and like good friends,

the Seal Sitters

watch over him.

Author's Note

Seals spend half their lives on the shores. Mothers usually give birth on land. There, they nurse and rest and warm up. But beaches are busy. That's why Seal Sitters watch over marine mammals. If you are near a coast that has seals, you can, too. If not, you can still help keep beaches clean by picking up trash and plastics like balloons.

If you see any seal pups on the beach, call your NOAA Marine Mammal Stranding Network. Keep dogs on leashes. Stay a safe distance away. Watch through your binoculars.

Be a good neighbor and share the land with seals like Leopard. It's fun. And you can save a life!

For more information, go to: www.leopardandsilkie.com.